CSS Flexbox

CSS FLEXBOX

Complete Guide with Images and Live Examples

Oluwatobi Sofela

C<8>DESWEETLY

First published by CodeSweetly 2023

CSS FLEXBOX

First edition. January 23, 2023.

www.codesweetly.com

C⟨8⟩DESWEETLY

Contents

Contents

Introduction

Welcome to Flexbox!

CSS Flexbox gives you the tools to create basic and advanced website layouts in flexible and responsive ways.

This book will use images and live examples to discuss everything you need to know to use Flexbox like a pro.

How This Book Can Help You Understand Flexbox

The best way to learn is through progressive practice. In other words, the easiest way to understand CSS Flexbox is to proactively try out Flexbox's concepts—rather than merely reading or watching videos about them.

As such, this book is intentionally examples-oriented to get you to practice as much as possible while learning the fundamental concepts of Flexbox.

Therefore, you will do yourself much favor by opening your text editor (such as VS Code) and trying out the concepts explained herein. By so doing, you will avoid being part of those stuck in "Tutorial Hell."

Book's Style

This book (CSS Flexbox) goes straight to the point to explain each Flexbox concept. It uses a short, simple, and direct explanation style. So, consider it as your quick and comprehensive reference guide to Flexbox.

Prerequisite

Familiarity with HTML and CSS will help you learn Flexbox better. So, to be better prepared for this book's content, it's best to be familiar with the elementary aspect of those two languages.

Using Live Examples

Whenever you come across a "Live Example[3]" text, it means there is an associated Stackblitz link where you will find a working demo.

You can visit the "Endnote" section at the end of this book to get the live demo's URL.

Note that the superscript number placed at the end of the "Live Example[3]" text references the text's associated endnote.

Questions and Comments

For questions and comments about this book, email contact@codesweetly.com or send me a direct message on Twitter (@oluwatobiss).

Let's Get It Started!

In the following chapter, you will learn what Flexbox is and why people use it.

Flexbox

Flexbox makes browsers display selected HTML elements as flexible <u>box models</u>[1].

Flexbox allows easy resizing and repositioning of a flexible container and its items one-dimensionally.

Note:

- "One-dimensionally" means Flexbox allows laying out box models in a row or column at a time. In other words, Flexbox cannot lay out box models in a row and column at the same time.

- Flexbox is sometimes called a flexible box layout module.

- Use the <u>grid layout module</u>[2] if you need to resize and reposition elements two-dimensionally.

Flex Container

A flex container (the large area below) is an <u>HTML element</u>[3] whose <u>display</u>[4] property's value is flex or inline-flex.

Flex Items

Flex items (the smaller boxes within the large container) are the direct children of a flex container.

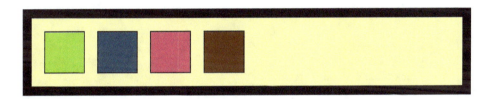

display: flex

flex tells browsers to display the selected HTML element as a block-level[5] flexible box model.

Converting a node to a flexible box model makes the element's direct children become flexible items.

Try it yourself

CSS

```css
section {
  display: flex;
  background-color: orange;
  margin: 10px;
  padding: 7px;
}

div {
  background-color: purple;
  color: white;
  margin: 5px;
  padding: 10px;
  border-radius: 5px;
}
```

HTML

```html
<section>
  <div>1</div>
  <div>2</div>
  <div>3</div>
</section>
<section>
  <div>4</div>
  <div>5</div>
  <div>6</div>
</section>
```

Live Example[7]

display: inline-flex

`inline-flex` tells browsers to display the selected HTML element as an inline-level[6] flexible box model.

The `display: inline-flex` directive only affects a box model and its direct children. It does not affect grandchildren nodes.

Try it yourself

CSS

```css
section {
    display: inline-flex;
    background-color: orange;
    margin: 10px;
    padding: 7px;
}

div {
    background-color: purple;
    color: white;
    margin: 5px;
    padding: 10px;
    border-radius: 5px;
}
```

HTML

```html
<section>
    <div>1</div>
    <div>2</div>
    <div>3</div>
</section>
<section>
    <div>4</div>
    <div>5</div>
    <div>6</div>
</section>
```

Live Example[8]

"Never be discouraged when you make progress, no matter how slow or small. Only be wary of standing still."

– John Mason

Flexible Containers Properties

A flexible container's properties specify how browsers should layout items within the flexible box model.

We define a flexible container's property on the flex container, not its items.

Types of flex container properties

1. flex-direction

2. flex-wrap

3. flex-flow

4. justify-content

5. align-items

6. align-content

flex-direction

flex-direction tells browsers the specific direction (row or column) they should lay out a flexible container's direct children.

In other words, flex-direction defines a flexbox's <u>main axis</u>[9].

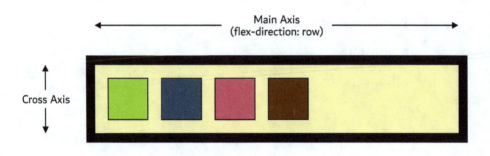

Try it yourself

CSS

```css
section {
  display: flex;
  flex-direction: column;
  background-color: orange;
  margin: 10px;
  padding: 7px;
}

div {
  background-color: purple;
  color: white;
  margin: 5px;
  padding: 10px;
  border-radius: 5px;
}
```

HTML

```html
<section>
  <div>1</div>
  <div>2</div>
  <div>3</div>
</section>
<section>
  <div>4</div>
  <div>5</div>
  <div>6</div>
</section>
```

Live Example[10]

YOUR FREE GIFT

As a thank you for buying my book, I would like to give you my
Git Cheat Sheet **100% FREE!**

DOWNLOAD IT HERE:

https://www.subscribepage.com/git-cheatsheet

flex-wrap Property

flex-wrap specifies whether browsers should wrap overflown flexible items onto multiple lines.

flex-wrap property's values

1. nowrap

2. wrap

3. wrap-reverse

flex-wrap: nowrap

nowrap forces all items within a flexible container into a single line (that is, row-wise or column-wise direction).

In other words, nowrap tells browsers not to wrap a flexible container's items.

Note: Suppose the total width (or height) of all the items in a flexible container is greater than the flexbox's width (or height). In such a case, nowrap will cause the elements to overflow out of the container.

Try it yourself

```css
section {
  width: 130px;
  display: flex;
  flex-wrap: nowrap;
  background-color: orange;
  margin: 10px;
  padding: 7px;
}

div {
  background-color: purple;
  color: white;
  margin: 5px;
  padding: 10px;
  border-radius: 5px;
}
```

```html
<section>
  <div>1</div>
  <div>2</div>
  <div>3</div>
</section>
<section>
  <div>4</div>
  <div>5</div>
  <div>6</div>
  <div>7</div>
  <div>8</div>
  <div>9</div>
  <div>10</div>
</section>
```

Live Example[11]

flex-wrap: wrap

`wrap` moves all overflow items within a flexible container to the next line.

In other words, `wrap` tells browsers to wrap a flexible container's overflow items.

Try it yourself

```css
CSS

section {
  width: 130px;
  display: flex;
  flex-wrap: wrap;
  background-color: orange;
  margin: 10px;
  padding: 7px;
}

div {
  background-color: purple;
  color: white;
  margin: 5px;
  padding: 10px;
  border-radius: 5px;
}
```

HTML

```
<section>
  <div>1</div>
  <div>2</div>
  <div>3</div>
</section>
<section>
  <div>4</div>
  <div>5</div>
  <div>6</div>
  <div>7</div>
  <div>8</div>
  <div>9</div>
  <div>10</div>
</section>
```

Live Example[12]

flex-wrap: wrap-reverse

`wrap-reverse` moves all overflow items within a flexible container to the next line in reverse order.

Note: `wrap-reverse` does the same thing as `wrap`—but in reverse order.

Try it yourself

```css
CSS

section {
  width: 130px;
  display: flex;
  flex-wrap: wrap-reverse;
  background-color: orange;
  margin: 10px;
  padding: 7px;
}

div {
  background-color: purple;
  color: white;
  margin: 5px;
  padding: 10px;
  border-radius: 5px;
}
```

HTML

```html
<section>
  <div>1</div>
  <div>2</div>
  <div>3</div>
</section>
<section>
  <div>4</div>
  <div>5</div>
  <div>6</div>
  <div>7</div>
  <div>8</div>
  <div>9</div>
  <div>10</div>
</section>
```

Live Example[13]

flex-flow Property

flex-flow is a shorthand for the flex-direction and flex-wrap properties.

In other words, instead of writing:

```css
CSS

section {
  display: flex;
  flex-direction: column;
  flex-wrap: wrap;
}
```

You can alternatively use the flex-flow property to shorten your code like so:

```css
CSS

section {
  display: flex;
  flex-flow: column wrap;
}
```

justify-content Property

justify-content specifies how browsers should position a flexible container's items along the flexbox's main axis.

justify-content property's values

1. flex-start

2. center

3. flex-end

4. space-between

5. space-around

6. space-evenly

justify-content: flex-start

flex-start aligns a flexible container's items with the main-start
edge of the flexbox's main axis.

Try it yourself

CSS

```css
section {
  display: flex;
  justify-content: flex-start;
  background-color: orange;
  margin: 10px;
}

div {
  border: 1px solid black;
  background-color: purple;
  color: white;
  padding: 10px;
  border-radius: 5px;
}
```

HTML

```html
<section>
  <div>1</div>
  <div>2</div>
  <div>3</div>
  <div>4</div>
</section>
```

Live Example[14]

justify-content: center

`center` aligns a flexible container's items to the center of the flexbox's main axis.

Try it yourself

CSS

```css
section {
  display: flex;
  justify-content: center;
  background-color: orange;
  margin: 10px;
}

div {
  border: 1px solid black;
  background-color: purple;
  color: white;
  padding: 10px;
  border-radius: 5px;
}
```

HTML

```html
<section>
  <div>1</div>
  <div>2</div>
  <div>3</div>
  <div>4</div>
</section>
```

Live Example[15]

justify-content: flex-end

flex-end aligns a flexible container's items with the main-end side of the flexbox's main axis.

Try it yourself

CSS

```css
section {
  display: flex;
  justify-content: flex-end;
  background-color: orange;
  margin: 10px;
}

div {
  border: 1px solid black;
  background-color: purple;
  color: white;
  padding: 10px;
  border-radius: 5px;
}
```

HTML

```html
<section>
  <div>1</div>
  <div>2</div>
  <div>3</div>
  <div>4</div>
</section>
```

Live Example[16]

justify-content: space-between

`space-between` does the following:

• aligns a flexible container's first item with the main-start edge of the flexbox's main axis.

• aligns the container's last item with the main-end edge of the flexbox's main axis.

• creates even spacing between each pair of items between the first and last item.

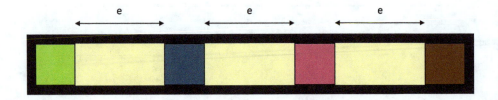

Try it yourself

CSS

```css
section {
  display: flex;
  justify-content: space-between;
  background-color: orange;
  margin: 10px;
}

div {
  border: 1px solid black;
  background-color: purple;
  color: white;
  padding: 10px;
  border-radius: 5px;
}
```

HTML

```html
<section>
  <div>1</div>
  <div>2</div>
  <div>3</div>
  <div>4</div>
</section>
```

Live Example[17]

justify-content: space-around

space-around assigns equal spacing to each side of a flexible container's items.

Therefore, the space before the first item and after the last element is half the width of the space between each pair of elements.

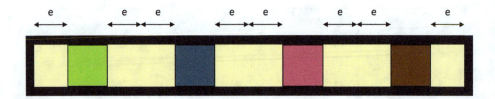

Try it yourself

CSS

```css
section {
  display: flex;
  justify-content: space-around;
  background-color: orange;
  margin: 10px;
}

div {
  border: 1px solid black;
  background-color: purple;
  color: white;
  padding: 10px;
  border-radius: 5px;
}
```

HTML

```html
<section>
  <div>1</div>
  <div>2</div>
  <div>3</div>
  <div>4</div>
</section>
```

Live Example[18]

justify-content: space-evenly

`space-evenly` assigns even spacing to both ends of a flexible container and between its items.

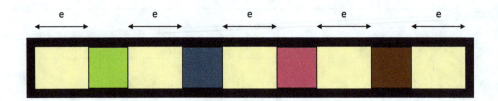

Try it yourself

CSS

```css
section {
  display: flex;
  justify-content: space-evenly;
  background-color: orange;
  margin: 10px;
}

div {
  border: 1px solid black;
  background-color: purple;
  color: white;
  padding: 10px;
  border-radius: 5px;
}
```

HTML

```html
<section>
  <div>1</div>
  <div>2</div>
  <div>3</div>
  <div>4</div>
</section>
```

Live Example[19]

"Victory is won not in miles but in inches. Win a little now, hold your ground, and later win a lot more."

– Louis L' Amour

align-items Property

`align-items` specifies how browsers should position a flexible container's items along the cross-axis of the flexbox.

align-items property's values

1. stretch

2. flex-start

3. center

4. flex-end

5. baseline

align-items: stretch

`stretch` stretches a flexible container's items to fill the flexbox's cross-axis.

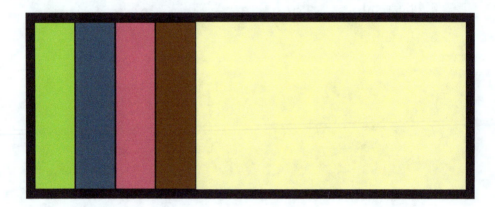

Try it yourself

CSS

```css
section {
  display: flex;
  align-items: stretch;
  background-color: orange;
  margin: 10px;
  height: 300px;
}

div {
  border: 1px solid black;
  background-color: purple;
  color: white;
  padding: 10px;
  border-radius: 5px;
}
```

HTML

```html
<section>
  <div>1</div>
  <div>2</div>
  <div>3</div>
  <div>4</div>
</section>
```

Live Example[20]

align-items: flex-start

flex-start aligns a flexible container's items with the cross-start edge of the flexbox's cross-axis.

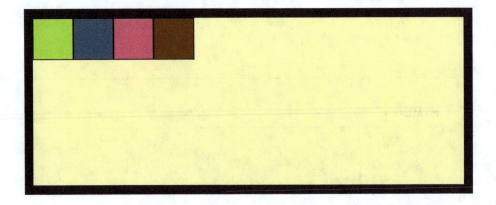

Try it yourself

CSS

```css
section {
  display: flex;
  align-items: flex-start;
  background-color: orange;
  margin: 10px;
  height: 300px;
}

div {
  border: 1px solid black;
  background-color: purple;
  color: white;
  padding: 10px;
  border-radius: 5px;
}
```

HTML

```html
<section>
  <div>1</div>
  <div>2</div>
  <div>3</div>
  <div>4</div>
</section>
```

Live Example[21]

align-items: center

center aligns a flexible container's items to the center of the flexbox's cross-axis.

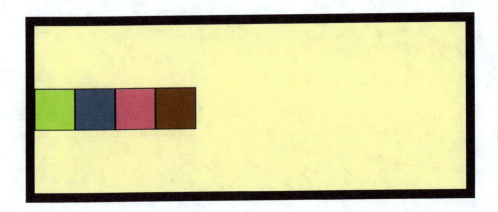

Try it yourself

CSS

```css
section {
  display: flex;
  align-items: center;
  background-color: orange;
  margin: 10px;
  height: 300px;
}

div {
  border: 1px solid black;
  background-color: purple;
  color: white;
  padding: 10px;
  border-radius: 5px;
}
```

HTML

```html
<section>
  <div>1</div>
  <div>2</div>
  <div>3</div>
  <div>4</div>
</section>
```

Live Example[22]

align-items: flex-end

flex-end aligns a flexible container's items with the cross-end edge of the flexbox's cross-axis.

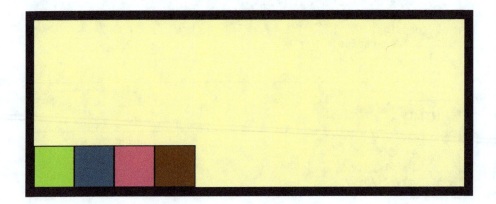

Try it yourself

CSS

```css
section {
  display: flex;
  align-items: flex-end;
  background-color: orange;
  margin: 10px;
  height: 300px;
}

div {
  border: 1px solid black;
  background-color: purple;
  color: white;
  padding: 10px;
  border-radius: 5px;
}
```

HTML

```html
<section>
  <div>1</div>
  <div>2</div>
  <div>3</div>
  <div>4</div>
</section>
```

Live Example[23]

align-items: baseline

baseline aligns a flexible container's items with the <u>baseline</u>[24] of the flexbox's cross-axis.

Try it yourself

CSS

```css
section {
  display: flex;
  align-items: baseline;
  background-color: orange;
  margin: 10px;
}

div {
  border: 1px solid black;
  background-color: purple;
  color: white;
  padding: 10px;
  border-radius: 5px;
}

.flex-item1 {
  font-size: 1.5rem;
}

.flex-item2 {
  font-size: 3rem;
}

.flex-item3 {
  font-size: 0.7rem;
}

.flex-item4 {
  font-size: 5rem;
}
```

HTML

```html
<section>
  <div class="flex-item1">1</div>
  <div class="flex-item2">2</div>
  <div class="flex-item3">3</div>
  <div class="flex-item4">4</div>
</section>
```

Live Example[25]

"Mount Everest, you beat me the first time, but I'll beat you the next time because you've grown all you are going to grow...and I'm still growing!"

– Edmund Hillary

align-content Property

`align-content` specify how browsers should position a flexible container's lines along the flexbox's cross-axis.

The `align-content` property does not affect a flexbox with only one line—for instance, a flexible container with `flex-wrap: nowrap`. In other words, `align-content` works only on flexboxes with multiple lines.

align-content property's values

1. stretch
2. flex-start
3. center
4. flex-end
5. space-between
6. space-around
7. space-evenly

align-content: stretch

`stretch` stretches the flexible container's lines to fill the flexbox's cross-axis.

Try it yourself

CSS

```css
section {
  display: flex;
  flex-wrap: wrap;
  align-content: stretch;
  background-color: orange;
  margin: 10px;
  width: 90px;
  height: 500px;
}

div {
  border: 1px solid black;
  background-color: purple;
  color: white;
  width: 30px;
  height: 30px;
  padding: 10px;
  border-radius: 5px;
}
```

HTML

```html
<section>
  <div>1</div>
  <div>2</div>
  <div>3</div>
  <div>4</div>
</section>
```

Live Example[26]

align-content: flex-start

flex-start aligns a flexible container's lines with the cross-start edge of the flexbox's cross-axis.

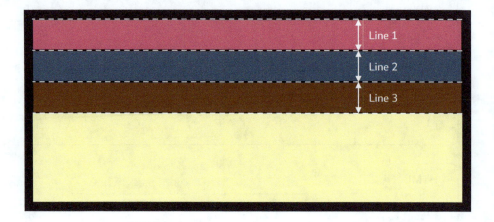

Try it yourself

CSS

```css
section {
  display: flex;
  flex-wrap: wrap;
  align-content: flex-start;
  background-color: orange;
  margin: 10px;
  width: 90px;
  height: 500px;
}

div {
  border: 1px solid black;
  background-color: purple;
  color: white;
  width: 30px;
  height: 30px;
  padding: 10px;
  border-radius: 5px;
}
```

HTML

```html
<section>
  <div>1</div>
  <div>2</div>
  <div>3</div>
  <div>4</div>
</section>
```

Live Example[27]

align-content: center

center aligns a flexible container's lines to the center of the flexbox's cross-axis.

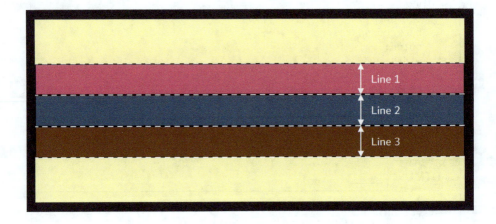

Try it yourself

CSS

```css
section {
  display: flex;
  flex-wrap: wrap;
  align-content: center;
  background-color: orange;
  margin: 10px;
  width: 90px;
  height: 500px;
}

div {
  border: 1px solid black;
  background-color: purple;
  color: white;
  width: 30px;
  height: 30px;
  padding: 10px;
  border-radius: 5px;
}
```

HTML

```html
<section>
  <div>1</div>
  <div>2</div>
  <div>3</div>
  <div>4</div>
</section>
```

Live Example[28]

align-content: flex-end

flex-end aligns a flexible container's lines with the cross-end edge of the flexbox's cross-axis.

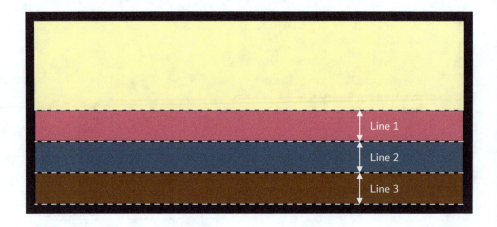

Try it yourself

CSS

```css
section {
  display: flex;
  flex-wrap: wrap;
  align-content: flex-end;
  background-color: orange;
  margin: 10px;
  width: 90px;
  height: 500px;
}

div {
  border: 1px solid black;
  background-color: purple;
  color: white;
  width: 30px;
  height: 30px;
  padding: 10px;
  border-radius: 5px;
}
```

HTML

```html
<section>
  <div>1</div>
  <div>2</div>
  <div>3</div>
  <div>4</div>
</section>
```

Live Example[29]

align-content: space-between

space-between does the following:

•   It aligns the flexbox's first line with the main-start edge of the flexible container's main axis.

•   It aligns the flexbox's last line with the main-end side of the flexible container's main axis.

•   It creates equal spacing between each pair of lines between the first and last line.

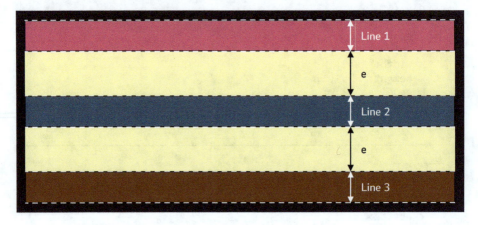

Try it yourself

CSS

```css
section {
  display: flex;
  flex-wrap: wrap;
  align-content: space-between;
  background-color: orange;
  margin: 10px;
  width: 90px;
  height: 500px;
}

div {
  border: 1px solid black;
  background-color: purple;
  color: white;
  width: 30px;
  height: 30px;
  padding: 10px;
  border-radius: 5px;
}
```

HTML

```html
<section>
  <div>1</div>
  <div>2</div>
  <div>3</div>
  <div>4</div>
</section>
```

Live Example[30]

align-content: space-around

space-around assigns equal spacing to each side of a flexible container's lines.

Therefore, the space before the first line and after the last one is half the width of the space between each pair of lines.

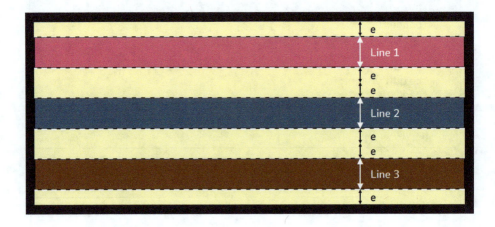

Try it yourself

```css
section {
  display: flex;
  flex-wrap: wrap;
  align-content: space-around;
  background-color: orange;
  margin: 10px;
  width: 90px;
  height: 500px;
}

div {
  border: 1px solid black;
  background-color: purple;
  color: white;
  width: 30px;
  height: 30px;
  padding: 10px;
  border-radius: 5px;
}
```

HTML

```html
<section>
  <div>1</div>
  <div>2</div>
  <div>3</div>
  <div>4</div>
</section>
```

Live Example[31]

align-content: space-evenly

`space-evenly` assigns even spacing to both ends of a flexible container and between its lines.

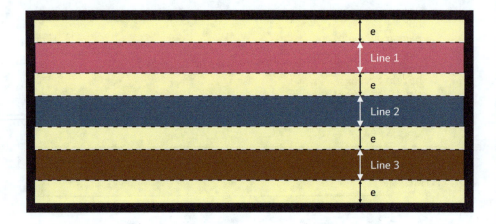

Try it yourself

CSS

```css
section {
  display: flex;
  flex-wrap: wrap;
  align-content: space-evenly;
  background-color: orange;
  margin: 10px;
  width: 90px;
  height: 500px;
}

div {
  border: 1px solid black;
  background-color: purple;
  color: white;
  width: 30px;
  height: 30px;
  padding: 10px;
  border-radius: 5px;
}
```

HTML

```html
<section>
  <div>1</div>
  <div>2</div>
  <div>3</div>
  <div>4</div>
</section>
```

Live Example[32]

Flexible Item's Properties

A flexible item's properties specify how browsers should layout a specified item within the flexible box model.

We define a flexible item's property on the flex item, not its container.

Types of flex items properties

1. align-self

2. order

3. flex-grow

4. flex-shrink

5. flex-basis

6. flex

align-self Property

`align-self` specifies how browsers should position selected flexible items along the flexbox's cross-axis.

`align-self` affects only the selected flexible item—not all the flexbox's items. It also overrides the `align-items` property.

align-self property's values

1. stretch
2. flex-start
3. center
4. flex-end
5. baseline

align-self: stretch

`stretch` stretches the selected flexible items to fill the flexbox's cross-axis.

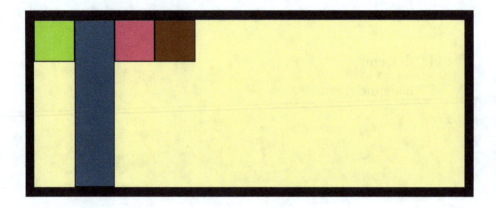

Try it yourself

CSS

```
section {
  display: flex;
  align-items: flex-start;
  background-color: orange;
  margin: 10px;
  height: 300px;
}

div {
  border: 1px solid black;
  background-color: purple;
  color: white;
  padding: 10px;
  border-radius: 5px;
}

.flex-item2 {
  align-self: stretch;
}
```

HTML

```
<section>
  <div class="flex-item1">1</div>
  <div class="flex-item2">2</div>
  <div class="flex-item3">3</div>
  <div class="flex-item4">4</div>
</section>
```

Live Example[33]

align-self: flex-start

flex-start aligns the selected flexible items with the cross-start edge of the flexbox's cross-axis.

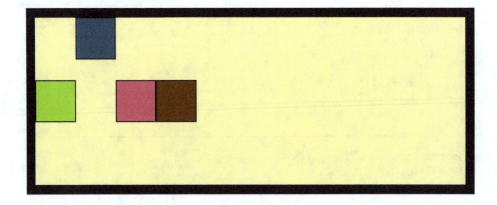

Try it yourself

CSS

```css
section {
  display: flex;
  align-items: center;
  background-color: orange;
  margin: 10px;
  height: 300px;
}

div {
  border: 1px solid black;
  background-color: purple;
  color: white;
  padding: 10px;
  border-radius: 5px;
}

.flex-item2 {
  align-self: flex-start;
}
```

HTML

```html
<section>
  <div class="flex-item1">1</div>
  <div class="flex-item2">2</div>
  <div class="flex-item3">3</div>
  <div class="flex-item4">4</div>
</section>
```

Live Example[34]

align-self: center

`center` aligns the selected flexible items to the center of the
flexbox's cross-axis.

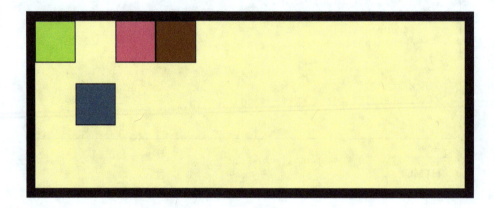

Try it yourself

CSS

```css
section {
  display: flex;
  align-items: flex-start;
  background-color: orange;
  margin: 10px;
  height: 300px;
}

div {
  border: 1px solid black;
  background-color: purple;
  color: white;
  padding: 10px;
  border-radius: 5px;
}

.flex-item2 {
  align-self: center;
}
```

HTML

```html
<section>
  <div class="flex-item1">1</div>
  <div class="flex-item2">2</div>
  <div class="flex-item3">3</div>
  <div class="flex-item4">4</div>
</section>
```

Live Example[35]

align-self: flex-end

flex-end aligns the selected flexible items with the cross-end edge of the flexbox's cross-axis.

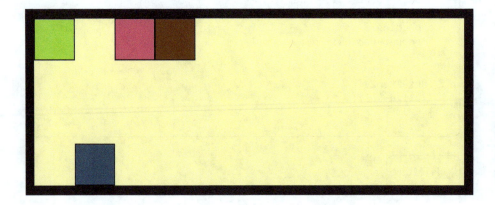

Try it yourself

CSS

```css
section {
  display: flex;
  align-items: flex-start;
  background-color: orange;
  margin: 10px;
  height: 300px;
}

div {
  border: 1px solid black;
  background-color: purple;
  color: white;
  padding: 10px;
  border-radius: 5px;
}

.flex-item2 {
  align-self: flex-end;
}
```

HTML

```html
<section>
  <div class="flex-item1">1</div>
  <div class="flex-item2">2</div>
  <div class="flex-item3">3</div>
  <div class="flex-item4">4</div>
</section>
```

Live Example[36]

align-self: baseline

`baseline` aligns the selected flexible items with the baseline of the flexbox's cross-axis.

Try it yourself

```css
CSS

section {
  display: flex;
  align-items: flex-end;
  background-color: orange;
  margin: 10px;
  height: 470px;
}

div {
  border: 1px solid black;
  background-color: purple;
  color: white;
  padding: 10px;
  border-radius: 5px;
}

.flex-item1 {
  font-size: 1.5rem;
}

.flex-item2 {
  font-size: 3rem;
  align-self: baseline;
}

.flex-item3 {
  font-size: 0.7rem;
}

.flex-item4 {
  font-size: 5rem;
}
```

HTML

```html
<section>
  <div class="flex-item1">1</div>
  <div class="flex-item2">2</div>
  <div class="flex-item3">3</div>
  <div class="flex-item4">4</div>
</section>
```

Live Example[37]

order Property

order changes a flexible item's default order (arrangement).

In other words, order allows you to reposition a flexbox's item without altering your HTML code's layout.

Use the order property with caution, as it prevents screen readers from accessing the correct reading order of an HTML document. Only use it if it is super important to use CSS to change the HTML code's layout.

But in most cases, it is best to rearrange the HTML code directly rather than using CSS.

Try it yourself

```html
HTML

<ul style="display: flex; flex-direction: column">
  <li style="order: 6">1</li>
  <li style="order: 4">2</li>
  <li style="order: 1">3</li>
  <li style="order: 7">4</li>
  <li style="order: 2">5</li>
  <li style="order: 5">6</li>
  <li style="order: 3">7</li>
</ul>
```

<u>Live Example</u>[38]

Note: The style="value" syntax, in the HTML snippet above, is the <u>inline CSS</u>[39] technique for styling HTML elements.

flex-grow Property

flex-grow tells browsers how much of the flexbox's left-over space they should add to the selected flexible item's size.

Note: A left-over space refers to the space remaining after browsers have deducted the sum of all flexible items' sizes from the flexbox's size.

Try it yourself

CSS

```css
section {
  display: flex;
  align-items: flex-start;
  background-color: orange;
  margin: 10px;
}

div {
  border: 1px solid black;
  background-color: purple;
  color: white;
  padding: 10px;
  border-radius: 5px;
}

.flex-item3 {
  flex-grow: 0.5;
}
```

HTML

```html
<section>
  <div class="flex-item1">1</div>
  <div class="flex-item2">2</div>
  <div class="flex-item3">3</div>
  <div class="flex-item4">4</div>
</section>
```

Live Example[40]

flex-shrink Property

flex-shrink tells browsers how much the specified flexible item should shrink when the sum of all items' sizes exceeds the flexbox's size.

In other words, suppose the flexbox's size is insufficient to fit the flexible items. In that case, browsers will shrink the items to fit the container.

Therefore, flex-shrink allows you to specify the shrinking factor of a flexible item.

Try it yourself

```css
section {
  display: flex;
  align-items: flex-start;
  background-color: orange;
  margin: 10px;
  width: 50%;
}

div {
  border: 1px solid black;
  background-color: purple;
  color: white;
  padding: 10px;
  border-radius: 5px;
  width: 40%;
}

.flex-item3 {
  flex-shrink: 0;
}
```

HTML

```
<section>
  <div class="flex-item1">1</div>
  <div class="flex-item2">2</div>
  <div class="flex-item3">3</div>
  <div class="flex-item4">4</div>
</section>
```

Live Example[41]

Note: Browsers will not shrink flexible items with a `flex-shrink` value of `0`.

flex-basis Property

flex-basis sets the initial length of a flexible item.

A flex-basis' value (other than auto) has higher specificity than width (or height). Therefore, suppose you define both for a flexible item. In that case, browsers will use flex-basis.

Try it yourself

CSS

```css
section {
    display: flex;
    align-items: flex-start;
    background-color: orange;
    margin: 10px;
}

div {
    border: 1px solid black;
    background-color: purple;
    color: white;
    padding: 10px;
    border-radius: 5px;
}

.flex-item3 {
    flex-basis: 100px;
}
```

HTML

```html
<section>
    <div class="flex-item1">1</div>
    <div class="flex-item2">2</div>
    <div class="flex-item3">3</div>
    <div class="flex-item4">4</div>
</section>
```

Live Example[42]

flex Property

flex is a shorthand for the flex-grow, flex-shrink, and flex-basis properties.

In other words, instead of writing:

```css
.flex-item3 {
  flex-grow: 0.5;
  flex-shrink: 0;
  flex-basis: 100px;
}
```

You can alternatively use the flex property to shorten your code like so:

```css
.flex-item3 {
  flex: 0.5 0 100px;
}
```

GET YOUR FREEBIE

If you didn't download it earlier, I would like you to have my Git
Cheat Sheet **100% FREE!**

<u>DOWNLOAD IT HERE</u>:

https://www.subscribepage.com/git-cheatsheet

Centering Elements with Flexbox

How to Center Elements Horizontally

1. Set the element's container's `display` property to `flex`.

2. Set the flexible container's `justify-content` property to `center`.

Try it yourself

CSS

```css
section {
  display: flex;
  justify-content: center;
  background-color: orange;
  width: 100%;
  height: 400px;
}

div {
  border: 1px solid black;
  background-color: purple;
  color: white;
  padding: 20px;
  border-radius: 5px;
  width: 50px;
  height: 50px;
}
```

HTML

```html
<section>
  <div></div>
</section>
```

Live Example[43]

How to Center Elements Vertically

1. Set the element's container's `display` property to `flex`.

2. Set the flexible container's `align-items` property to `center`.

Try it yourself

```css
section {
  display: flex;
  align-items: center;
  background-color: orange;
  width: 100%;
  height: 400px;
}

div {
  border: 1px solid black;
  background-color: purple;
  color: white;
  padding: 20px;
  border-radius: 5px;
  width: 50px;
  height: 50px;
}
```

CSS

```html
<section>
  <div></div>
</section>
```

HTML

Live Example[44]

How to Center Elements Horizontally and Vertically

1. Set the element's container's `display` property to `flex`.

2. Set the flexible container's `justify-content` and `align-items` properties to `center`.

Try it yourself

CSS

```css
section {
  display: flex;
  justify-content: center;
  align-items: center;
  background-color: orange;
  width: 100%;
  height: 400px;
}

div {
  border: 1px solid black;
  background-color: purple;
  color: white;
  padding: 20px;
  border-radius: 5px;
  width: 50px;
  height: 50px;
}
```

HTML

```html
<section>
  <div></div>
</section>
```

Live Example[45]

Endnotes

[1] Box model (https://codesweetly.com/css-box-model)

[2] Grid layout module (https://codesweetly.com/css-grid-explained)

[3] HTML element (https://codesweetly.com/web-tech-terms-h#html-element)

[4] CSS display property (https://codesweetly.com/css-display-property)

[5] Block-level HTML elements (https://developer.mozilla.org/en-US/docs/Web/HTML/Block-level_elements)

[6] Inline-level HTML elements (https://developer.mozilla.org/en-US/docs/Web/HTML/Inline_elements)

[7] display: flex live example (https://stackblitz.com/edit/js-gctvuc?file=style.css

[8] display: inline-flex live example (https://stackblitz.com/edit/js-ksagv8?file=style.css)

[9] main axis (https://codesweetly.com/css-flex-direction-property#main-axis-vs-cross-axis-whats-the-difference)

[10] flex-direction live example (https://stackblitz.com/edit/js-jtpqir?file=style.css)

[11] flex-wrap: nowrap live example (https://stackblitz.com/edit/js-yn6yw8?file=style.css)

[12] flex-wrap: wrap live example (https://stackblitz.com/edit/js-78ez1m?file=style.css)

[13] flex-wrap: wrap-reverse live example (https://stackblitz.com/edit/js-eyqxtf?file=style.css)

[14] justify-content: flex-start live example (https://stackblitz.com/edit/js-ma7svj?file=style.css)

[15] justify-content: center live example (https://stackblitz.com/edit/js-jfzcwc?file=style.css)

Endnotes

[16] justify-content: flex-end live example (https://stackblitz.com/edit/js-iyhlbr?file=style.css)

[17] justify-content: space-between live example (https://stackblitz.com/edit/js-dylovp?file=style.css)

[18] justify-content: space-around live example (https://stackblitz.com/edit/js-t6wpcj?file=style.css)

[19] justify-content: space-evenly live example (https://stackblitz.com/edit/js-p67eh8?file=style.css)

[20] align-items: stretch live example (https://stackblitz.com/edit/js-ezugee?file=style.css)

[21] align-items: flex-start live example (https://stackblitz.com/edit/js-cjzhj2?file=style.css)

[22] align-items: center live example (https://stackblitz.com/edit/js-ywexqr?file=style.css)

[23] align-items: flex-end live example (https://stackblitz.com/edit/js-bwdeyz?file=style.css)

[24] Baseline (https://stackoverflow.com/a/34611670/11841906)

[25] align-items: baseline live example (https://stackblitz.com/edit/js-xxvj57?file=style.css)

[26] align-content: stretch live example (https://stackblitz.com/edit/js-dway6n?file=style.css)

[27] align-content: flex-start live example (https://stackblitz.com/edit/js-c9pzbc?file=style.css)

[28] align-content: center live example (https://stackblitz.com/edit/js-j3poyu?file=style.css)

[29] align-content: flex-end live example (https://stackblitz.com/edit/js-cmaz6z?file=style.css)

[30] align-content: space-between live example (https://stackblitz.com/edit/js-kltdwx?file=style.css)

Endnotes

[31] align-content: space-around live example (https://stackblitz.com/edit/js-kx9gdy?file=style.css)

[32] align-content: space-evenly live example (https://stackblitz.com/edit/js-eevqoj?file=style.css)

[33] align-self: stretch live example (https://stackblitz.com/edit/js-o5qr62?file=style.css)

[34] align-self: flex-start live example (https://stackblitz.com/edit/js-6uianm?file=style.css)

[35] align-self: center live example (https://stackblitz.com/edit/js-tazf2p?file=style.css)

[36] align-self: flex-end live example (https://stackblitz.com/edit/js-7bec4q?file=style.css)

[37] align-self: baseline live example (https://stackblitz.com/edit/js-wmawek?file=style.css)

[38] CSS order property live example (https://stackblitz.com/edit/js-hmz9my?file=index.html)

[39] Inline CSS (https://codesweetly.com/inline-vs-internal-vs-external-css#what-is-an-inline-css)

[40] CSS flex-grow property live example (https://stackblitz.com/edit/js-grtdo1?file=style.css)

[41] CSS flex-shrink property live example (https://stackblitz.com/edit/js-h2numw?file=style.css)

[42] CSS flex-basis property live example (https://stackblitz.com/edit/js-kwcche?file=style.css)

[43] Centering element horizontally live example (https://stackblitz.com/edit/js-trl46e?file=style.css)

[44] Centering element vertically live example (https://stackblitz.com/edit/js-tm1don?file=style.css)

[45] Centering element horizontally and vertically live example (https://stackblitz.com/edit/js-ryzwmq?file=style.css)

Other CodeSweetly Book...

React Explained Clearly

Available at Amazon

(https://www.amazon.com/dp/B09KYGDQYW)

C<8>DESWEETLY

CodeSweetly exists specifically to help make coding so easy and fun to learn.

Visit codesweetly.com to learn web technology topics with simplified articles, images, and cheat sheets.